A Detailed Instant Pot Recipe Book

Best Detailed Book with Practical Recipes, for Eat Healthy Foods Anyone Can Cook, without Sacrificing Taste

Adrian Marvin

Table of Contents

Introduction

Instant pot is a pressure cooker, also stir-fry, stew, and cook rice, cook vegetables and chicken. It's an all-in-one device, so you can season chicken and cook it in the same pan, for example. In most cases, instant pot meals can be served in less than an hour.

Cooking less time is due to the pressure cooking function that captures the steam generated by the liquid cooking environment (including liquids released from meat and vegetables), boosts the pressure and pushes the steam back.

But don't confuse with traditional pressure cookers. The instant pot, unlike the pressure cooker used by grandparents, eliminates the risk of safety with a lid that locks and remains locked until pressure is released.

Even when cooking time is over in the instant pot, you need to take an additional step-to release the pressure.

There are two ways to relieve pressure. Due to the natural pressure release, the lid valve remains in the sealing position and the pressure will naturally dissipate over time. This process takes 20 minutes to over an hour, depending on what is cooked. Low fluidity foods (such as chicken wings) take less time than high fluidity foods such as soups and marinades.

Another option is manual pressure release (also called quick release). Now you need to carefully move the valve to the ventilation position and see that the steam rises slowly and the pressure is released. This Directions is much faster, but foods with high liquid content, such as soups, take about 15 minutes to manually relieve pressure.

Which option should I use? Take into account that even if natural pressure is released, the instant pot is still under pressure. This means that the food will continue to cook while the instant pot is in sealed mode. Manual pressure relief is useful when the dishes are well cooked and need to be stopped as soon as possible.

If the goal is to prepare meals quickly, set the cooking time for dishes that are being cooked in an instant pop and release the pressure manually after the time has passed.

Instant pots (called "Instapot" by many) are one of our favorite cookware because they can handle such a wide range of foods almost easily. Instant pots range from those that work on the basics of pressure cooking to those that can be sterilized using Suicide video or some models can be controlled via Wi-Fi.

In addition, if you want to expand the range of kitchenware, the Instant Pot brand has released an air fryer that can be used to make rotisserie chicken and homemade beef jerky. There is also an independent accumulator device that can be used in instant pots to make fish, steaks and more.

The current icon instant pot works like a pressure cooker and uses heat and steam to quickly cook food. Everything from perfect carnitas to boiled eggs was cooked, but not all ingredients and

DIRECTIONSs work. Here are few foods that should not be cooked in classic instant pots.

Instant pots are not pressure fryer and are not designed to handle the high temperatures required to heat cooking oils like crispy fried chicken. Of course, the instant pot is great for dishes like Carnitas, but after removing the meat from the instant pot, to get the final crispness in the meat, transfer it to a frying pan for a few minutes or to an oven top and hot Crispy in the oven.

As with slow cookers, dairy products such as cheese, milk, and sour cream will pack into instant pots using pressure cooking settings or slow cooking settings. Do not add these ingredients after the dish are cooked or create a recipe in Instapot.

There are two exceptions. One is when making yogurt. This is merely possible if you are using an instant pot recipe. The other is only when making cheesecake and following an instant pot recipe.

Although you can technically cook pasta in an instant pot, gummy may appear and cooking may be uneven. To be honest, unless you have a choice, cooking pasta in a stove pot is just as fast and easy and consistently gives you better cooked pasta.

Instead of baking the cake in an instant pot, steam it. The cake is moist-it works for things like bread pudding-but there is no good skin on the cake or on the crunchy edge everyone fights with a baked brownie. However, let's say your desire is to build a close-up or a simple dessert with your family; you can get a damp sponge in about 30 minutes, except during the DIRECTIONS time.

Canning, a technique for cooking and sealing food in a jar, is often done in a pressure cooker. Therefore, it is recommended to create a batch of jam, pickles or jelly in Instapot. Please do not.

With an instant pot, you can't monitor the temperature of what you can, like a normal pressure cooker. In canning, it is important to cook and seal the dishes correctly. Incorrect cooking and sealing can lead to the growth of bacteria that can cause food poisoning.

If you want to avoid canning in an instant pot, some newer models, such as Duo Plus, have a sterilization setting that can clean kitchen items such as baby bottles, bottles and cookware.

Instant Pot Pressure Cooker Safety Tips

Instant Pot is a very safe pressure cooker consisting of various safety mechanisms. do not worry. It will not explode immediately. Most accidents are caused by user errors and can be easily avoided. To further minimize the possibility of an accident, we have compiled a list of safety tips.

1 Don't leave it alone

It is not recommended to leave home while cooking an instant pot. If you have to leave it alone, make sure it is under pressure and no steam is coming out.

2 Do not use KFC in instant pot

Do not fry in an instant pot or other pressure cooker.

KFC uses a commercial pressure fryer specially made to fry chicken (the latest one that operates at 5 PSI). Instant pots (10.5-11.6 PSI) are specially made to make our lives easier.

3 water intake!

Instant pots require a minimum of 1 1/2 cup liquid (Instant Pot Official Number) 1 cup liquid to reach and maintain pressure.

The liquid can be a combination of gravy, vinegar, water, chicken etc.

4 half full or half empty

The max line printed on the inner pot of the instant pot is not for pressure cooking.

For pressure cooking: up to 2/3 full

Food for pressure cooking that expands during cooking (grains, beans, dried vegetables, etc.): up to 1/2

5 Not a facial steamer

Deep cleaning is not performed even if the pressure cooker steam is used once.

When opening, always tilt the lid away from you. Wear waterproof and heat-resistant silicone gloves especially when performing quick release.

6 never use power

In situations of zero, you should try to force open the lid of the instant pot pressure cooker, unless you want to prevent a light saber from hitting your face.

7 Wash Up & Checkout

If you want to be secured, wash the lid after each use and clean the anti-block shield and inner pot. Make sure that the gasket (silicon seal ring) is in good shape and that there is no food residue in the anti-block shield before use.

Usually silicone seal rings should be replaced every 18-24 months. It is always advisable to keep extra things.

Do not purchase a sealing ring from a third party because it is an integral part of the safety features of the instant ring.

Using sealing rings that have not been tested with instant pot products can create serious safety concerns."

Before use, make sure that the sealing ring is securely fixed to the sealing ring rack and the anti-block shield is properly attached to the vapor discharge pipe.

A properly fitted sealing ring can be moved clockwise or counterclockwise in the sealing ring rack with little force.

With instant pots, the whole family can cook meals in less than 30 minutes. Cooked dishes such as rice, chicken, beef stew, sauce, yakitori can be cooked for 30-60 minutes from the beginning to the end. And yes, you can bake bread in an instant pot.

Old and ketogenic diet fans love instant pots for their ability to `` roast '' meat in such a short time, but vegetarians and vegans that can quickly cook dishes such as pumpkin soup, baked potatoes and marinated potato chilis, also highly appreciated oatmeal cream and macaroni and cheese.

Even dried beans, which usually require overnight cooking, can be prepared in 30 minutes to make spicy hummus.

Tamarind Yogurt Dip

Preparation Time: 10 minutes

Cooking Time: 20 minutes

Servings: 4

Ingredients:

2 cups yogurt

2 red onions, chopped

2 tablespoons coconut oil, melted

1 cup tamarind chutney

1 cup mint, chopped

2 tomatoes, chopped

2 teaspoons red chili powder

2 tablespoons cumin seeds

Directions:

In your instant pot, combine the yogurt with the onions and other ingredients, close it and cook on High for 20 minutes.

Naturally release the pressure for 10 minutes, whisk the mix, divide into bowls and serve as a party dip.

Nutrition:

Calories – 244

Protein – 2.5 g.

Fat – 4.4 g.

Carbs – 11 g.

Cashew Paneer Dip

Preparation Time: 5 minutes

Cooking Time: 10 minutes

Servings: 4

Ingredients:

8 ounces paneer, cubed

1 cup cashews, chopped

8 tablespoons water

2 tablespoons vinegar

½ teaspoon turmeric powder

A pinch of salt and black pepper

1 and ½ teaspoons sweet paprika

1 tablespoon lime juice

1 cup water

Directions:

In a bowl, combine every ingredient except for the water, whisk well and transfer to a ramekin. Transfer the water in the instant pot, add the trivet inside, put the ramekin inside, close it and cook on High for 10 minutes.

Release the pressure naturally for 5 minutes and serve as a dip.

Nutrition:

Calories – 232

Protein – 5 g.

Fat – 11.1 g.

Carbs – 6.6 g.

Capsicum Bell Masala

Preparation Time: 10 minutes

Cooking Time: 15 minutes

Servings: 4

Ingredients:

1 pound green bell peppers, deseeded and roughly
cubed

2 tablespoons vegetable oil

½ teaspoon cumin seeds

1 tablespoon coconut powder

1 and ½ tablespoon sesame seed powder

2 teaspoons coriander powder

2 teaspoons fennel seed powder

½ teaspoon chili powder

¼ teaspoon turmeric powder

1 teaspoon lemon juice

¼ cup veggie stock

Directions:

In your instant pot, combine the bell peppers with
the oil, cumin seeds and the rest of the

ingredients, close it and cook on High for 15 minutes.

Naturally release the pressure for 10 minutes, transfer the mix to small bowls and serve cold as an appetizer.

Nutrition:

Calories – 240

Protein – 6 g.

Fat – 4.6 g.

Carbs – 7.6 g.

Bell Almonds Dip

Preparation Time: 5 minutes

Cooking Time: 20 minutes

Servings: 4

Ingredients:

2 red bell peppers, chopped

4 tomatoes, chopped

12 garlic cloves, minced

20 almonds, chopped

1 tablespoon white wine vinegar

2 tablespoons vegetable oil

Salt and black pepper to the taste

Directions:

Put the instant poton Sauté mode, add the oil ,heat it up, add the garlic and the almonds and sauté for 5 minutes.

Add the bell peppers and the other ingredients, close it and cook on High for 15 minutes.

Naturally release the pressure for 5 minutes, blend the mix using an immersion blender, divide into bowls and serve.

Nutrition:

Calories – 160

Protein – 7 g.

Fat – 9 g.

Carbs – 7.6 g.

Shrimp Bowls

Preparation Time: 30 minutes

Cooking Time: 6 minutes

Servings: 4

Ingredients:

1 pound shrimp, peeled and deveined

1 tablespoon vegetable oil

Juice of 1 lime

½ tablespoon cilantro, chopped

¼ cup curd

1 teaspoon garlic, minced

½ teaspoon garam masala

¼ teaspoon chili powder

Salt to the taste

¼ teaspoon turmeric powder

Directions:

In a bowl, add in the shrimp with the oil, lime juice and the other ingredients, toss and keep in the fridge for 25 minutes.

Transfer everything to your instant pot, close it and cook on High for 6 minutes.

Naturally release the pressure for 5 minutes, transfer the shrimp mixture to small bowls and serve as an appetizer.

Nutrition:

Calories – 170

Protein – 6 g.

Fat – 11.9 g.

Carbs – 9.5 g.

Pepper Shrimp Mix

Preparation Time: 10 minutes

Cooking Time: 6 minutes

Servings: 4

Ingredients:

1 pound shrimp, peeled and deveined

2 teaspoons red pepper flakes

½ teaspoon cumin, ground

½ teaspoon turmeric powder

Salt to the taste

½ teaspoon turmeric powder

1 tablespoon vegetable oil

Directions:

In your instant pot, combine the shrimp with the pepper flakes and the other ingredients, close it and cook on High for 6 minutes.

Naturally release the pressure for 10 minutes, divide the shrimp into bowls and serve as an appetizer.

Nutrition:
Calories – 280

Protein – 9 g.

Fat – 13.4 g.

Carbs – 7 g.

Easy Buttery Brussels Sprouts

Preparation Time: 5 minutes

Cooking Time: 5 minutes

Servings: 4

Ingredients:

1 tablespoon butter

1/2 cup shallots, chopped

3/4 pound whole Brussels sprouts

Sea salt, to taste

1/4 teaspoon ground black pepper

1/2 cup water

1/2 cup chicken stock

Directions:

Press the "Sauté" button to heat up your Instant Pot. Once hot, melt the butter and sauté the shallots until tender and translucent.

Add the remaining ingredients to the Instant Pot. Secure the lid. Choose "Manual" mode and High pressure; cook for 4 minutes. Once done, do a quick pressure release; cautiously remove the lid.

.

Transfer Brussels sprouts to a serving platter.
Serve with cocktail sticks and enjoy!

Nutrition:

Calories – 68

Protein – 3.5 g.

Fat – 3.3 g.

Carbs – 7.8 g.

Easy Spinach Dip

Preparation Time: 3 minutes

Cooking Time: 2 minutes

Servings: 10

Ingredients:

1 pound spinach

4 ounces Cottage cheese, at room temperature

4 ounces Cheddar cheese, grated

1 teaspoon garlic powder

1/2 teaspoon shallot powder

1/2 teaspoon celery seeds

1/2 teaspoon fennel seeds

1/2 teaspoon cayenne pepper

Salt and black pepper, to taste

Directions:

Add all ingredients to your Instant Pot.

Secure the lid. Choose "Manual" mode and High pressure; cook for 1 minute. Once done, do a quick pressure release; cautiously remove the lid.

.

Serve warm or at room temperature. Bon appétit!

Nutrition:

Calories – 43

Protein – 4.1 g.

Fat – 1.7 g.

Carbs – 3.5 g.

Asparagus with Chervil Dip

Preparation Time: 3 minutes

Cooking Time: 2 minutes

Servings: 6

Ingredients:

1 ½ pounds asparagus spears, trimmed

1/2 cup sour cream

1/2 cup mayonnaise

2 tablespoons fresh chervil

2 tablespoons scallions, chopped

1 teaspoon garlic, minced

Salt, to taste

Directions:

Add 1 cup of water and a steamer basket to you Instant Pot.

Secure the lid. Choose "Manual" mode and High pressure; cook for 1 minute. Once done, do a quick pressure release; cautiously remove the lid.

.

Then, thoroughly combine the remaining ingredients to make your dipping sauce. Serve your asparagus with the dipping sauce on the side.

Bon appétit!

Nutrition:

Calories – 116

Protein – 4.5 g.

Fat – 8.5 g.

Carbs – 6.9 g.

Cheesy Mustard Greens Dip

Preparation Time: 5 minutes

Cooking Time: 5 minutes

Servings: 10

Ingredients:

2 tablespoons butter, melted

20 ounces mustard greens

2 bell peppers, chopped

1 white onion, chopped

1 teaspoon garlic, minced

1 cup chicken stock

8 ounces Neufchâtel cheese, crumbled

1/2 teaspoon dried thyme

1/2 teaspoon dried dill

1/2 teaspoon turmeric powder

Sea salt and black pepper, to taste

3/4 cup Romano cheese, preferably freshly grated

Directions:

Add the butter, mustard greens, bell peppers, onion, and garlic to the Instant Pot.

Secure the lid. Choose "Manual" mode and High pressure; cook for 3 minutes. Once done, do a quick pressure release; cautiously remove the lid.

.

Then, add the remaining ingredients and press the "Sauté" button. Let it simmer until the cheese is melted; then, gently stir this mixture until everything is well incorporated.

Serve with your favorite low-carb dippers.

Nutrition:

Calories – 153

Protein – 8.7 g.

Fat – 10.6 g.

Carbs – 7 g.

Asian-Style Cocktail Sausage

Preparation Time: 5 minutes

Cooking Time: 5 minutes

Servings: 8

Ingredients:

1 teaspoon sesame oil

20 mini cocktail sausages

1/2 cup tomato puree

1/2 cup chicken stock

1 tablespoon dark soy sauce

1/3 teaspoon ground black pepper

1/2 teaspoon paprika

Himalayan salt, to taste

1/2 teaspoon mustard seeds

1/2 teaspoon fennel seeds

1/4 teaspoon fresh ginger root, grated

1 teaspoon garlic paste

Directions:

Simply throw all ingredients into your Instant Pot. Secure the lid. Choose "Manual" mode and High pressure; cook for 4 minutes. Once done, do a quick pressure release; cautiously remove the lid.

.

Serve with cocktail sticks and enjoy!

Nutrition:

Calories – 330

Protein – 22.7 g.

Fat – 24.8 g.

Carbs – 2.7 g.

Colorful Stuffed Mushrooms

Preparation Time: 5 minutes

Cooking Time: 5 minutes

Servings: 5

Ingredients:

1 tablespoon butter, softened

1 shallot, chopped

2 cloves garlic, minced

1 ½ cups Cottage cheese, at room temperature

1/2 cup Romano cheese, grated

1 red bell pepper, chopped

1 green bell pepper, chopped

1 jalapeno pepper, minced

1/2 teaspoon dried basil

1/2 teaspoon dried oregano

1/2 teaspoon dried rosemary

10 medium-sized button mushrooms, stems removed

Directions:

Press the "Sauté" button to heat up your Instant Pot. Once hot, melt the butter and sauté the shallots until tender and translucent.

Stir in the garlic and cook an additional 30 seconds or until aromatic. Now, add the remaining ingredients, except for the mushroom caps, and stir to combine well.

Then, fill the mushroom caps with this mixture. Add 1 cup of water and a steamer basket to you Instant Pot. Arrange the stuffed mushrooms in the steamer basket.

Secure the lid. Choose "Manual" mode and High pressure; cook for 5 minutes. Once done, do a quick pressure release; cautiously remove the lid.
.

Arrange the stuffed mushroom on a serving platter and serve. Enjoy!

Nutrition:

Calories – 151

Protein – 11.9 g.

Fat – 9.2 g.

Carbs – 6 g.

Dad's Cocktail Meatballs

Preparation Time: 5 minutes

Cooking Time: 10 minutes

Servings: 6

Ingredients:

1/2 pound ground pork

1 pound ground beef

1/2 cup Romano cheese, grated

1/2 cup pork rinds, crushed

1 egg, beaten

sea salt and black pepper, to taste

1 teaspoon granulated garlic

1/2 teaspoon cayenne pepper

1/2 teaspoon dried basil

1/4 cup milk, lukewarm

1 ½ cups BBQ sauce

Directions:

Thoroughly combine ground meat, cheese, pork rinds, egg, salt, black pepper, garlic, cayenne pepper, basil, and milk in the mixing bowl.

Then, roll the mixture into 20 meatballs.

Pour BBQ sauce into your Instant Pot. Now, add the meatballs and secure the lid.

Choose "Manual" mode and High pressure; cook for 8 minutes. Once done, do a quick pressure release; cautiously remove the lid. . Bon appétit!

Nutrition:

Calories – 384

Protein – 38.4 g.

Fat – 22.2 g.

Carbs – 6.1 g.

Herbed and Caramelized Mushrooms

Preparation Time: 5 minutes

Cooking Time: 5 minutes

Servings: 4

Ingredients:

2 tablespoons butter, melted

20 ounces button mushrooms, brushed clean

2 cloves garlic, minced

1 teaspoon dried basil

1 teaspoon dried rosemary

1 teaspoon dried sage

1 bay leaf

Sea salt, to taste

1/2 teaspoon freshly ground black pepper

1/2 cup water

1/2 cup broth, preferably homemade

1 tablespoon soy sauce

1 tablespoon fresh parsley leaves, roughly chopped

Directions:

Press the "Sauté" button to heat up your Instant Pot. Once hot, melt the butter and sauté the mushrooms and garlic until aromatic.

Add seasonings, water, and broth. Add garlic, oregano, mushrooms, thyme, basil, bay leaves, veggie broth, and salt and pepper to your instant pot.

Secure the lid. Choose "Manual" mode and High pressure; cook for 5 minutes. Once done, do a quick pressure release; cautiously remove the lid. .

Arrange your mushrooms on a serving platter and serve with cocktail sticks. Bon appétit!

Nutrition:

Calories – 91

Protein – 5.2 g.

Fat – 6.4 g.

Carbs – 5.5 g.

Colby Cheese Dip with Peppers

Preparation Time: 5 minutes

Cooking Time: 5 minutes

Servings: 8

Ingredients:

1 tablespoon butter

2 red bell peppers, sliced

1 teaspoon red Aleppo pepper flakes

1 cup cream cheese, room temperature

2 cups Colby cheese, shredded

1 teaspoon sumac

2 garlic cloves, minced

1 cup chicken broth

Salt and ground black pepper, to taste

Directions:

Press the "Sauté" button to heat up your Instant Pot. Once hot, melt the butter. Sauté the peppers until just tender.

Add the remaining ingredients; gently stir to combine.

Secure the lid. Choose "Manual" mode and High pressure; cook for 3 minutes. Once done, do a quick pressure release; cautiously remove the lid.

.

Serve with your favorite keto dippers. Bon appétit!

Nutrition:

Calories – 237

Protein – 10.2 g.

Fat – 20.6 g.

Carbs – 3.1 g.

Party Chicken Drumettes

Preparation Time: 5 minutes

Cooking Time: 10 minutes

Servings: 8

Ingredients:

2 pounds chicken drumettes

1 stick butter

1 tablespoon coconut aminos

Sea salt and black pepper, to taste

1/2 teaspoon dried dill weed

1/2 teaspoon dried basil

1 teaspoon hot sauce

1 tablespoon fish sauce

1/2 cup tomato sauce

1/2 cup water

Directions:

Add all ingredients to your Instant Pot.

Secure the lid. Choose "Poultry" mode and High pressure; cook for 10 minutes. Once done cooking,use a natural pressure release; carefully remove the lid.

Serve at room temperature and enjoy!

Nutrition:

Calories – 237

Protein – 10.2 g.

Fat – 20.6 g.

Carbs – 3.1 g.

Cheesy Cauliflower Balls

Preparation Time: 5 minutes

Cooking Time: 20 minutes

Servings: 8

Ingredients:

1 head of cauliflower, broken into florets

2 tablespoons butter

sea salt and white pepper, to taste

1/2 teaspoon cayenne pepper

1 garlic clove, minced

1/2 cup Parmesan cheese, grated

1 cup Asiago cheese, shredded

2 tablespoons fresh chopped chives, minced

2 eggs, beaten

Directions:

Add 1 cup of water and a steamer basket to the Instant Pot. Now, add cauliflower to the steamer basket.

Secure the lid. Choose "Manual" mode and High pressure; cook for 3 minutes. Once done, do a quick pressure release; cautiously remove the lid.

.

Transfer the cauliflower to a food processor. Add
the remaining ingredients; process until
everything is well incorporated.

Shape the mixture into balls. Bake in the
preheated oven at 400 degrees F for 18 minutes.
Bon appétit!

Nutrition:

Calories – 157

Protein – 8.9 g.

Fat – 12.1 g.

Carbs – 3.6 g.

Crave-Worthy Balsamic Baby Carrots

Preparation Time: 5 minutes

Cooking Time: 5 minutes

Servings: 8

Ingredients:

28 ounces baby carrots

1 cup chicken broth

1/2 cup water

1/2 stick butter

2 tablespoons balsamic vinegar

Coarse sea salt, to taste

1/2 teaspoon red pepper flakes, crushed

1/2 teaspoon dried dill weed

Directions:

Add all ingredients to your Instant Pot.

Secure the lid. Choose "Manual" mode and High pressure; cook for 3 minutes. Once done, do a quick pressure release; cautiously remove the lid.

.

Transfer to a nice serving bowl and serve. Enjoy!

Nutrition:

Calories – 94

Protein – 1.4 g.

Fat – 6.1 g.

Carbs – 8.9 g.

Super Bowl Pizza Dip

Preparation Time: 5 minutes

Cooking Time: 5 minutes

Servings: 10

Ingredients:

10 ounces cream cheese

10 ounces Pepper-Jack cheese

1 pound tomatoes, pureed

10 ounces pancetta, chopped

1 cup green olives, pitted and halved

1/2 teaspoon garlic powder

1 teaspoon dried oregano

1 cup chicken broth

4 ounces Mozzarella cheese, thinly sliced

Directions:

Combine cream cheese, Pepper-Jack cheese, tomatoes, pancetta, olives, garlic, powder, and oregano in your Instant Pot.

Secure the lid. Choose "Manual" mode and High pressure; cook for 4 minutes. Once done, do a quick pressure release; cautiously remove the lid.

.

Top with Mozzarella cheese; cover and let it sit in the residual heat. Serve warm or at room temperature. Bon appétit!

Nutrition:

Calories – 280

Protein – 20.6 g.

Fat – 20.4 g.

Carbs – 3.7 g.

Minty Party Meatballs

Preparation Time: 5 minutes

Cooking Time: 10 minutes

Servings: 6

Ingredients:

1/2 pound ground pork

1/2 pound ground turkey

2 eggs

1/3 cup almond flour

Sea salt and black pepper, to taste

2 garlic cloves, minced

1 cup Romano cheese, grated

1 teaspoon dried basil

1/2 teaspoon dried thyme

1/4 cup minced fresh mint, plus more for garnish

1/2 cup beef bone broth

1/2 cup tomatoes, puréed

2 tablespoons scallions

Directions:

Thoroughly combine all ingredients, except for broth, tomatoes, and scallions in a mixing bowl.

Shape the mixture into 2-inch meatballs and reserve.

Add beef bone broth, tomatoes, and scallions to your Instant Pot. Place the meatballs in this sauce. Secure the lid. Choose "Manual" mode and High pressure; cook for 8 minutes. Once done, do a quick pressure release; cautiously remove the lid. . Bon appétit!

Nutrition:

Calories – 280

Protein – 20.6 g.

Fat – 20.4 g.

Carbs – 3.7 g.

Chicken Wings Italiano

Preparation Time: 5 minutes

Cooking Time: 15 minutes

Servings: 12

Ingredients:

4 pounds chicken wings cut into sections

1/2 cup butter, melted

1 tablespoon Italian seasoning mix

1/2 teaspoon onion powder

1/2 teaspoon garlic powder

1 teaspoon paprika

1/2 teaspoon coarse sea salt

1/2 teaspoon ground black pepper

1 cup Parmigiano-Reggiano cheese, shaved

2 eggs, lightly whisked

Directions:

Add chicken wings, butter, Italian seasoning mix, onion powder, garlic powder, paprika, salt, and black pepper to your Instant Pot.

Secure the lid. Choose "Poultry" mode and High pressure. Cook the chicken wings for 10 minutes.

Once done cooking,use a natural pressure release; carefully remove the lid.

Mix Parmigiano-Reggiano cheese with eggs. Spoon this mixture over the wings.

Secure the lid. Choose "Manual" mode and High pressure; cook for 4 minutes longer. Once done, do a quick pressure release; cautiously remove the lid. Bon appétit!

Nutrition:

Calories – 443

Protein – 33.2 g.

Fat – 30.8 g.

Carbs – 6.2 g.

Snacks

Prosciutto-Wrapped Parmesan Asparagus

Preparation Time: 10 minutes

Cooking Time: 10 minutes

Servings: 4

Ingredients:

1-pound asparagus

12 (0.5-ounce) slices prosciutto

1 tablespoon coconut oil, melted

2 teaspoons lemon juice

⅛ teaspoon red pepper flakes

⅓ cup grated Parmesan cheese

2 tablespoons salted butter, melted

Directions:

On a clean work surface, place an asparagus spear onto a slice of prosciutto.

Drizzle with coconut oil and lemon juice. Sprinkle red pepper flakes and Parmesan across asparagus.

Roll prosciutto around asparagus spear. Place into the instant pot basket.

Adjust the temperature to 375°F and set the timer for 10 minutes.

Drizzle the asparagus roll with butter before serving.

Nutrition:

Calories: 263

Protein: 13.9 g

Fiber: 2.4 g

Net carbohydrates: 4.3 g

Fat: 20.2 g

Sodium: 368 mg

Carbohydrates: 6.7 g

Sugar: 2.2 g

Bacon-Wrapped Jalapeño Poppers

Preparation Time: 15 minutes

Cooking Time: 12 minutes

Servings: 4

Ingredients:

jalapeños (about 4" long each)

3 ounces full-fat cream cheese

⅓ cup shredded medium Cheddar cheese

¼ teaspoon garlic powder

12 slices sugar-free bacon

Directions:

Cut the tops off of the jalapeños and slice down the center lengthwise into two pieces. Use a knife to carefully remove white membrane and seeds from peppers.

In a large microwave-safe bowl, place cream cheese, Cheddar, and garlic powder. Microwave for 30 seconds and stir. Spoon cheese mixture into hollow jalapeños.

Wrap a slice of bacon around each jalapeño half, completely covering pepper. Place into the instant pot basket.

Adjust the temperature to 400°F and set the timer for 12 minutes.

Turn the peppers halfway through the cooking time. Serve warm.

Nutrition:

Calories: 246

Protein: 14.4 g

Fiber: 0.6 g

Net carbohydrates: 2.0 g

Fat: 17.9 g

Sodium: 625 mg

Carbohydrates: 2.6 g

Sugar: 1.6 g

Garlic Parmesan Chicken Wings

Preparation Time: 5 minutes

Cooking Time: 25 minutes

Servings: 4

Ingredients:

2 pounds raw chicken wings

1 teaspoon pink Himalayan salt

½ teaspoon garlic powder

1 tablespoon baking powder

4 tablespoons unsalted butter, melted

⅓ cup grated Parmesan cheese

¼ teaspoon dried parsley

Directions:

In a large bowl, place chicken wings, salt, ½ teaspoon garlic powder, and baking powder, then toss. Place wings into the instant pot basket. Adjust the temperature to 400°F and set the timer for 25 minutes.

Toss the basket two or three times during the cooking time.

In a small bowl, combine butter, Parmesan, and parsley.

Remove wings from the fryer and place into a clean large bowl. Pour the butter mixture over the wings and toss until coated. Serve warm.

Nutrition:

Calories: 565

Protein: 41.8 g

Fiber: 0.1 g

Net carbohydrates: 2.1 g

Fat: 42.1 g

Sodium: 1,067 mg

Carbohydrates: 2.2 g

Sugar: 0.0 g

Spicy Buffalo Chicken Dip

Preparation Time: 10 minutes

Cooking Time: 10 minutes

Servings: 4

Ingredients:

1 cup cooked, diced chicken breast

8 ounces full-fat cream cheese, softened

½ cup buffalo sauce

⅓ cup full-fat ranch dressing

⅓ cup chopped pickled jalapeños

1½ cups shredded medium Cheddar cheese, divided

2 scallions, sliced on the bias

Directions:

Place chicken into a large bowl. Add cream cheese, buffalo sauce, and ranch dressing. Stir until the sauces are well mixed and mostly smooth. Fold in jalapeños and 1 cup Cheddar.

Pour the mixture into a 4-cup round baking dish and place remaining Cheddar on top. Place dish into the instant pot basket.

Adjust the temperature to 350°F and set the timer for 10 minutes.

When done, the top will be brown and the dip bubbling. Top with sliced scallions. Serve warm.

Nutrition:

Calories: 472

Protein: 25.6 g

Fiber: 0.6 g

Net carbohydrates: 8.5 g

Fat: 32.0 g

Sodium: 1,532 mg

Carbohydrates: 9.1 g

Sugar: 7.4 g

Bacon Jalapeño Cheese Bread

Preparation Time: 10 minutes

Cooking Time: 15 minutes

Servings: 8 sticks

Ingredients:

2 cups shredded mozzarella cheese

¼ cup grated Parmesan cheese

¼ cup chopped pickled jalapeños

2 large eggs

slices sugar-free bacon, cooked and chopped

Directions:

Mix all ingredients in a large bowl. Cut a piece of parchment to fit your instant pot basket.

Dampen your hands with a bit of water and press out the mixture into a circle. You may need to separate this into two smaller cheese breads, depending on the size of your fryer.

Place the parchment and cheese bread into the instant pot basket.

Adjust the temperature to 320°F and set the timer for 15 minutes.

Carefully flip the bread when 5 minutes remain.

When fully cooked, the top will be golden brown.

Serve warm.

Nutrition:

Calories: 273

Protein: 20.1 g

Fiber: 0.1 g

Net carbohydrates: 2.1 g

Fat: 18.1 g

Sodium: 749 mg

Carbohydrates: 2.3 g

Sugar: 0.7 g

Pizza Rolls

Preparation Time: 15 minutes

Cooking Time: 10 minutes

Servings: 24

Ingredients:

2 cups shredded mozzarella cheese

½ cup almond flour

2 large eggs

72 slices pepperoni

(1-ounce) mozzarella string cheese sticks, cut into

3 pieces each

2 tablespoons unsalted butter, melted

¼ teaspoon garlic powder

½ teaspoon dried parsley

2 tablespoons grated Parmesan cheese

Directions:

In a large microwave-safe bowl, place mozzarella and almond flour. Microwave for 1 minute.

Remove bowl and mix until ball of dough forms. Microwave additional 30 seconds if necessary.

Crack eggs into the bowl and mix until smooth dough ball forms. Wet your hands with water and knead the dough briefly.

Tear off two large pieces of parchment paper and spray one side of each with nonstick cooking spray. Place the dough ball between the two sheets, with sprayed sides facing dough. Use a rolling pin to roll dough out to ¼" thickness.

Use a knife to slice into 24 rectangles. On each rectangle place 3 pepperoni slices and 1 piece string cheese.

Fold the rectangle in half, covering pepperoni and cheese filling. Pinch or roll sides closed. Cut a piece of parchment to fit your instant pot basket and place it into the basket. Put the rolls onto the parchment.

Adjust the temperature to 350°F and set the timer for 10 minutes.

After 5 minutes, open the fryer and flip the pizza rolls. Restart the fryer and continue cooking until pizza rolls are golden.

In a small bowl, place butter, garlic powder, and parsley. Brush the mixture over cooked pizza rolls and then sprinkle with Parmesan. Serve warm.

Nutrition:

Calories: 333

Protein: 20.7 g

Fiber: 0.8 g

Net carbohydrates: 2.5 g

Fat: 24.0 g

Sodium: 708 mg

Carbohydrates: 3.3 g

Sugar: 0.9 g

Bacon Cheeseburger Dip

Preparation Time: 20 minutes

Cooking Time: 10 minutes

Servings: 6

Ingredients:

ounces full-fat cream cheese

¼ cup full-fat mayonnaise

¼ cup full-fat sour cream

¼ cup chopped onion

1 teaspoon garlic powder

1 tablespoon Worcestershire sauce

1¼ cups shredded medium Cheddar cheese, divided

½ pound cooked 80/20 ground beef

slices sugar-free bacon, cooked and crumbled

2 large pickle spears, chopped

Directions:

Place cream cheese in a large microwave-safe bowl and microwave for 45 seconds. Stir in mayonnaise, sour cream, onion, garlic powder, Worcestershire sauce, and 1 cup Cheddar. Add cooked ground beef and bacon. Sprinkle remaining Cheddar on top.

Place in 6" bowl and put into the instant pot basket.

Adjust the temperature to 400°F and set the timer for 10 minutes.

Dip is done when top is golden and bubbling.

Sprinkle pickles over dish. Serve warm.

Nutrition:

Calories: 457

Protein: 21.6 g

Fiber: 0.2 g

Net carbohydrates: 3.6 g

Fat: 35.0 g

Sodium: 589 mg

Carbohydrates: 3.8 g

Sugar: 2.2 g

Pork Rind Tortillas

Preparation Time: 10 minutes

Cooking Time: 5 minutes

Servings: 4

Ingredients:

1 ounce pork rinds

¾ cup shredded mozzarella cheese

2 tablespoons full-fat cream cheese

1 large egg

Directions:

Place pork rinds into food processor and pulse until finely ground.

Place mozzarella into a large microwave-safe bowl. Break cream cheese into small pieces and add them to the bowl. Microwave for 30 seconds, or until both cheeses are melted and can easily be stirred together into a ball. Add ground pork rinds and egg to the cheese mixture.

Continue stirring until the mixture forms a ball. If it cools too much and cheese hardens, microwave for 10 more seconds.

Separate the dough into four small balls. Place each ball of dough between two sheets of parchment and roll into ¼" flat layer.

Place tortillas into the instant pot basket in single layer, working in batches if necessary.

Adjust the temperature to 400°F and set the timer for 5 minutes.

Tortillas will be crispy and firm when fully cooked. Serve immediately.

Nutrition:

Calories: 145

Protein: 10.7 g

Fiber: 0.0 g

Net carbohydrates: 0.8 g

Fat: 10.0 g

Sodium: 291 mg

Carbohydrates: 0.8 g

Sugar: 0.5 g

Mozzarella Sticks

Preparation Time: 1 hour

Cooking Time: 10 minutes

Servings: Yields 12 sticks (3 per serving)

Ingredients:

(1-ounce) mozzarella string cheese sticks

½ cup grated Parmesan cheese

½ ounce pork rinds, finely ground

1 teaspoon dried parsley

2 large eggs

Directions:

Place mozzarella sticks on a cutting board and cut in half. Freeze 45 minutes or until firm. If freezing overnight, remove frozen sticks after 1 hour and place into airtight zip-top storage bag and place back in freezer for future use.

In a large bowl, mix Parmesan, ground pork rinds, and parsley.

In a medium bowl, whisk eggs.

Dip a frozen mozzarella stick into beaten eggs and then into Parmesan mixture to coat. Repeat with remaining sticks. Place mozzarella sticks into the instant pot basket.

Adjust the temperature to 400°F and set the timer for 10 minutes or until golden.

Serve warm.

Nutrition:

Calories: 236

Protein: 19.2 g

Fiber: 0.0 g

Net carbohydrates: 4.7 g

Fat: 13.8 g

Sodium: 609 mg

Carbohydrates: 4.7 g

Sugar: 1.1 g

Bacon-Wrapped Onion Rings

Preparation Time: 5 minutes

Cooking Time: 10 minutes

Servings: 4

Ingredients:

1 large onion, peeled

1 tablespoon sriracha

slices sugar-free bacon

Directions:

Slice onion into ¼"-thick slices. Brush sriracha over the onion slices. Take two slices of onion and wrap bacon around the rings. Repeat with remaining onion and bacon. Place into the instant pot basket.

Adjust the temperature to 350°F and set the timer for 10 minutes.

Use tongs to flip the onion rings halfway through the cooking time. When fully cooked, bacon will be crispy. Serve warm.

Nutrition:

Calories: 105

Protein: 7.5 g

Fiber: 0.6 g

Net carbohydrates: 3.7 g

Fat: 5.9 g

Sodium: 401 mg

Carbohydrates: 4.3 g

Sugar: 2.3 g

Mini Sweet Pepper Poppers

Preparation Time: 15 minutes

Cooking Time: 8 minutes

Servings: 16

Ingredients:

mini sweet peppers

ounces full-fat cream cheese, softened

slices sugar-free bacon, cooked and crumbled

¼ cup shredded pepper jack cheese

Directions:

Remove the tops from the peppers and slice each one in half lengthwise. Use a small knife to remove seeds and membranes.

In a small bowl, mix cream cheese, bacon, and pepper jack.

Place 3 teaspoons of the mixture into each sweet pepper and press down smooth. Place into the fryer basket.

Adjust the temperature to 400°F and set the timer for 8 minutes.

Serve warm.

Nutrition:

Calories: 176

Protein: 7.4 g

Fiber: 0.9 g

Net carbohydrates: 2.7 g

Fat: 13.4 g

Sodium: 309 mg

Carbohydrates: 3.6 g

Sugar: 2.2 g

Spicy Spinach Artichoke Dip

Preparation Time: 10 minutes

Cooking Time: 10 minutes

Servings: 6

Ingredients:

ounces frozen spinach, drained and thawed

1 (14-ounce) can artichoke hearts, drained and
chopped

¼ cup chopped pickled jalapeños

ounces full-fat cream cheese, softened

¼ cup full-fat mayonnaise

¼ cup full-fat sour cream

½ teaspoon garlic powder

¼ cup grated Parmesan cheese

1 cup shredded pepper jack cheese

Directions:

Mix all ingredients in a 4-cup baking bowl. Place
into the instant pot basket.

Adjust the temperature to 320°F and set the timer
for 10 minutes.

Remove when brown and bubbling. Serve warm.

Nutrition:

Calories: 226

Protein: 10.0 g

Fiber: 3.7 g

Net carbohydrates: 6.5 g

Fat: 15.9 g

Sodium: 776 mg

Carbohydrates: 10.2 g

Sugar: 3.4 g

Personal Mozzarella Pizza Crust

Preparation Time: 5 minutes

Cooking Time: 10 minutes

Servings: 1

Ingredients:

½ cup shredded whole-milk mozzarella cheese

2 tablespoons blanched finely ground almond flour

1 tablespoon full-fat cream cheese

1 large egg white

Directions:

Place mozzarella, almond flour, and cream cheese in a medium microwave-safe bowl. Microwave for 30 seconds. Stir until smooth ball of dough forms. Add egg white and stir until soft round dough forms.

Press into a 6" round pizza crust.

Cut a piece of parchment to fit your instant pot basket and place crust on parchment. Place into the instant pot basket.

Adjust the temperature to 350°F and set the timer for 10 minutes.

Flip after 5 minutes and at this time place any desired toppings on the crust. Continue cooking until golden. Serve immediately.

Nutrition:

Calories: 314

Protein: 19.9 g

Fiber: 1.5 g

Net carbohydrates: 3.6 g

Fat: 22.7 g

Sodium: 457 mg

Carbohydrates: 5.1 g

Sugar: 1.8 g

Garlic Cheese Bread

Preparation Time: 10 minutes

Cooking Time: 10 minutes

Servings: 2

Ingredients:

1 cup shredded mozzarella cheese

¼ cup grated Parmesan cheese

1 large egg

½ teaspoon garlic powder

Directions:

Mix all Ingredients in a large bowl. Cut a piece of parchment to fit your instant pot basket. Press the mixture into a circle on the parchment and place into the instant pot basket.

Adjust the temperature to 350°F and set the timer for 10 minutes.

Serve warm.

Nutrition:

Calories: 258

Protein: 19.2 g

Fiber: 0.1 g

Net carbohydrates: 3.6 g

Fat: 16.6 g

Sodium: 612 mg

Carbohydrates: 3.7 g

Sugar: 0.7 g

Crustless Three-Meat Pizza

Preparation Time: 5 minutes

Cooking Time: 5 minutes

Servings: 1

Ingredients:

½ cup shredded mozzarella cheese

slices pepperoni

¼ cup cooked ground sausage

2 slices sugar-free bacon, cooked and crumbled

1 tablespoon grated Parmesan cheese

2 tablespoons low-carb, sugar-free pizza sauce,
for dipping

Directions:

Cover the bottom of a 6" cake pan with
mozzarella. Place pepperoni, sausage, and bacon
on top of cheese and sprinkle with Parmesan.

Place pan into the instant pot basket.

Adjust the temperature to 400°F and set the timer
for 5 minutes.

Remove when cheese is bubbling and golden.

Serve warm with pizza sauce for dipping.

Nutrition:

Calories: 466

Protein: 28.1 g

Fiber: 0.5 g

Net carbohydrates: 4.7 g

Fat: 34.0 g

Sodium: 1,446 mg

Carbohydrates: 5.2 g

Sugar: 1.6 g

Bacon Snack

Preparation Time: 15 minutes

Cooking Time: 10 minutes

Servings: 4

Ingredients:

1cup dark chocolate; melted

4bacon slices; halved

A pinch of pink salt

Directions:

Dip each bacon slice in some chocolate, sprinkle pink salt over them.

Put them in your instant pot's basket and cook at 350°F for 10 minutes

Nutrition:

Calories: 151

Fat: 4g

Fiber: 2g

Carbs: 4g

Protein: 8g

Shrimp Snack

Preparation Time: 15 minutes

Cooking Time: 10 minutes

Servings: 4

Ingredients:

1lb. shrimp; peeled and deveined

¼ cup olive oil

3garlic cloves; minced

¼ tsp. cayenne pepper

Juice of ½ lemon

A pinch of salt and black pepper

Directions:

In a pan that fits your instant pot, mix all the ingredients, toss,

Introduce in the fryer and cook at 370°F for 10 minutes

Servings as a snack

Nutrition:

 Calories: 242

Fat: 14g

Fiber: 2g

Carbs: 3g,Protein: 17g

Avocado Wraps

Preparation Time: : 20 minutes

Cooking Time: 15 minutes

Servings: 4

Ingredients:

2avocados, peeled, pitted and cut into 12 wedges

1tbsp. ghee; melted

12bacon strips

Directions:

Wrap each avocado wedge in a bacon strip, brush them with the ghee.

Put them in your instant pot's basket and cook at 360°F for 15 minutes

Servings as an appetizer

Nutrition:

Calories: 161

Fat: 4g

Fiber: 2g

Carbs: 4g

Protein: 6g

Cheesy Meatballs

Preparation Time: 30 minutes

Cooking Time: 30 minutes

Servings: 16

Ingredients:

1lb. 80/20 ground beef.

3oz.low-moisture, whole-milk mozzarella, cubed

1large egg.

½ cup low-carb, no-sugar-added pasta sauce.

¼ cup grated Parmesan cheese.

¼ cup blanched finely ground almond flour.

¼ tsp. onion powder.

tsp. dried parsley.

½ tsp. garlic powder.

Directions:

Take a large bowl, add ground beef, almond flour, parsley, garlic powder, onion powder and egg.

Fold ingredientstogether until fully combined

Form the mixture into 2-inch balls and use your thumb or a spoon to create an indent in the center of each meatball. Place a cube of cheese in the center and form the ball around it.

Place the meatballs into the instant pot, working in batches if necessary. Adjust the temperature to 350 Degrees F and set the timer for 15 minutes Meatballs will be slightly crispy on the outside and fully cooked when at least 180 Degrees F internally.

When they are finished cooking, toss the meatballs in the sauce and sprinkle with grated Parmesan for serving.

Nutrition:

Calories: 447

Protein: 29.6g

Fiber: 1.8g

Fat: 29.7g

Carbs: 5.4g

Tuna Appetizer

Preparation Time: 15 minutes

Cooking Time: 10 minutes

Servings: 2

Ingredients:

1lb. tuna, skinless; boneless and cubed

3scallion stalks; minced

1chili pepper; minced

2tomatoes; cubed

1tbsp. coconut aminos

2tbsp. olive oil

1tbsp. coconut cream

1tsp. sesame seeds

Directions:

In a pan that fits your instant pot, mix all the ingredientsexcept the sesame seeds, toss, introduce in the fryer and cook at 360°F for 10 minutes

Divide into bowls and serve as an appetizer with sesame seeds sprinkled on top.

Nutrition:

Calories: 231

Fat: 18g

Fiber: 3g

Carbs: 4g

Protein: 18g

Cheese And Leeks Dip

Preparation Time: 17 minutes

Cooking Time: 12 minutes

Servings: 6

Ingredients:

2spring onions; minced

4leeks; sliced

¼ cup coconut cream

3tbsp. coconut milk

2tbsp. butter; melted

Salt and white pepper to the taste

Directions:

In a pan that fits your instant pot, mix all the ingredients and whisk them well.

Introduce the pan in the fryer and cook at 390°F for 12 minutes. Divide into bowls and serve

Nutrition:

Calories: 204

Fat: 12g

Fiber: 2g

Carbs: 4g

Protein: 14g

Cucumber Salsa

Preparation Time: 10 minutes

Cooking Time: 5 minutes

Servings: 4

Ingredients:

1½ lb. cucumbers; sliced

2red chili peppers; chopped.

2tomatoes cubed

2spring onions; chopped.

1tbsp. balsamic vinegar

2tbsp. ginger; grated

A drizzle of olive oil

Directions:

In a pan that fits your instant pot, mix all the ingredients, toss, introduce in the fryer and cook at 340°F for 5 minutes

Divide into bowls and serve cold as an appetizer.

Nutrition:

Calories: 150

Fat: 2g

Fiber: 1g

Carbs: 2g,Protein: 4g

Chicken Cubes

Preparation Time: 25 minutes

Cooking Time: 20 minutes

Servings: 4

Ingredients:

1lb. chicken breasts, skinless; boneless and cubed

2eggs

¾ cup coconut flakes

2tsp. garlic powder

Cooking spray

Salt and black pepper to taste.

Directions:

Put the coconut in a bowl and mix the eggs with garlic powder, salt and pepper in a second one. Dredge the chicken cubes in eggs and then in coconut and arrange them all in your instant pot's basket

Grease with cooking spray, cook at 370°F for 20 minutes. Arrange the chicken bites on a platter and serve as an appetizer.

Nutrition:

Calories: 202

Fat: 12g

Fiber: 2g

Carbs: 4g

Protein: 7g

Salmon Spread

Preparation Time: 11 minutes

Cooking Time: 6 minutes

Servings: 4

Ingredients:

8oz. cream cheese, soft

½ cup coconut cream

4oz. smoked salmon, skinless; boneless and minced

2tbsp. lemon juice

1tbsp. chives; chopped.

A pinch of salt and black pepper

Directions:

Take a bowl and mix all the ingredients and whisk them really well.

Transfer the mix to a ramekin, place it in your instant pot's basket and cook at 360°F for 6 minutes

Nutrition:

Calories: 180

Fat: 7g

Fiber: 1g

Carbs: 5g

Protein: 7g

Crustless Pizza

Preparation Time: 10 minutes

Cooking Time: 5 minutes

Servings: 1

Ingredients:

2slices sugar-free bacon; cooked and crumbled

7slices pepperoni

½ cup shredded mozzarella cheese

¼ cup cooked ground sausage

2tbsp. low-carb, sugar-free pizza sauce, for dipping

1tbsp. grated Parmesan cheese

Directions:

Cover the bottom of a 6-inch cake pan with mozzarella. Place pepperoni, sausage and bacon on top of cheese and sprinkle with Parmesan Place pan into the instant pot basket. Adjust the temperature to 400 Degrees F and set the timer for 5 minutes.

Remove when cheese is bubbling and golden.

Serve warm with pizza sauce for dipping

Nutrition:

Calories: 466

Protein: 28.1g

Fiber: 0.5g

Fat: 34.0g

Carbs: 5.2g

Olives And Zucchini Cakes

Preparation Time: 17 minutes

Cooking Time: 6 minutes

Servings: 6

Ingredients:

3spring onions; chopped.

½ cup kalamata olives, pitted and minced

3zucchinis; grated

½ cup parsley; chopped.

½ cup almond flour

1egg

Cooking spray

Salt and black pepper to taste.

Directions:

Take a bowl and mix all the ingredientsexcept the
cooking spray, stir well and shape medium cakes
out of this mixture

Place the cakes in your instant pot's basket,
grease them with cooking spray and cook at 380°F
for 6 minutes on each side. Serve as an appetizer.

Nutrition:

Calories: 165

Fat: 5g

Fiber: 2g

Carbs: 3g

Protein: 7g

Fluffy Strawberry Muffins

Preparation Time: 10 minutes

Cooking Time: 25 minutes

Servings: 12

Ingredients:

1 ½ cups almond flour

1 tsp baking powder

½ tsp xanthan gum

½ cup Lakanto monk fruit sweetener

2 eggs, beaten

1 tsp vanilla extract

½ tsp almond extract

3 tbsps. unsalted butter

3 tbsps. unsweetened vanilla almond milk

½ cup chopped strawberries

Directions:

Preheat the oven to 350° F.

Take the 2 eggs and beat them with vanilla extract, melted butter, almond extract, and unsweetened almond milk until creamy and smooth. This should take around 2 minutes.

In another bowl, mix sweetener, xanthan gum, baking powder, and almond flour.

Combine the dry and wet ingredients and mix well; you should not have any lumps.

Add the chopped strawberries to the batter and use a plastic spatula to fold them in.

Take a muffin tin and put cupcake liners in each of the molds. Fill ¾ of each mold with the batter.

Bake for 20-25 minutes. You can check if they are done by inserting a toothpick into the center of a muffin; the toothpick will come out clean if they are done.

Nutrition:

Calories 144

Carbs 2g

Protein 5g

Fat 13g

Fiber 2g

Paleo Blueberry Muffins

Preparation Time: 10 minutes

Cooking Time: 20 minutes

Servings: 12

Ingredients:

½ cup coconut flour

4 ½ tbsps. coconut oil

6 organic eggs

4 tbsps. milk

½ tsp apple cider vinegar

½ tsp baking soda

¼ tsp baking powder

1 tsp cinnamon

¼ tsp sea salt

2 tbsps. raw honey

½ cup blueberries

Directions:

Preheat the oven to 400° F.

Combine all wet ingredients(coconut oil, eggs, milk, apple cider vinegar, honey) in a medium-sized bowl.

In another bowl, mix all the dry ingredients(coconut flour, baking soda, baking powder, cinnamon, sea salt).

Add dry ingredientsto the bowl of the wet ingredients and combine them well.

Add blueberries to the batter and stir thoroughly. The blueberries should be evenly spread throughout the batter.

Pour batter into baking cups or a muffin tin. If you are using a muffin tin, make sure to use cupcake liners.

Bake for 10-15 minutes, or until golden brown.

Nutrition:

Calories 210

Carbs 6g

Sugar 2g

Protein 7g

Fat 19g

Fiber 3g

Orange Cardamom Muffins With Coconut Butter Glaze

Preparation Time: 10 minutes

Cooking Time: 30 minutes

Servings: 6

Ingredients:

2 cups blanched almond flour

3 large eggs

1 tbsp orange zest

¼ cup fresh orange juice

½ tsp cardamom

¼ tsp salt

1 tsp baking powder

2 tsp Stevia sweetener

2 tbsps. coconut oil, melted

For coconut butter glaze:

1 tbsp coconut oil

¼ cup coconut butter

½ tbsp Stevia sweetener

Directions:

Preheat the oven to 350° F.

In a medium-sized bowl, whisk eggs, orange zest, and orange juice.

In another bowl, combine the dry ingredients(almond flour, cardamom, salt, baking powder, sweetener).

Combine dry ingredientswith the wet ingredientsby folding them in gently, then stir to form an even better.

After this, add the coconut oil and fold through again.

Line muffin tin with paper liners and pour ⅓ cup of batter into each muffin cup.

Bake for 25-30 minutes.

When done, let the cupcakes cool down for at least 10 minutes.

While your cupcakes are cooling, start working on the glaze. Start by melting the coconut oil and coconut butter on the stove.

Stir this mixture until it is smooth and take it off the stove, then add the sweetener.

Once your cupcakes have fully cooled, drizzle the glaze on top of them.

Nutrition:

Calories 219

Carbs 7g

Sugar 2g

Protein 5.5g

Fat 20g

Conclusion

When you are on a diet trying to lose weight or manage a condition, you will be strictly confined to follow an eating plan. Such plans often place numerous demands on individuals: food may need to be boiled, other foods are forbidden, permitting you only to eat small portions and so on.

On the other hand, a lifestyle such as the Mediterranean diet is entirely stress-free. It is easy to follow because there are almost no restrictions. There is no time limit on the Mediterranean diet because it is more of a lifestyle than a diet. You do not need to stop at some point but carry on for the rest of your life. The foods that you eat under the Mediterranean model include unrefined cereals, white meats, and the occasional dairy products.

The Mediterranean lifestyle, unlike other diets, also requires you to engage with family and friends and share meals together. It has been noted that communities around the Mediterranean spend between one and two hours enjoying their meals.

This kind of bonding between family members or friends helps bring people closer together, which helps foster closer bonds hence fewer cases of depression, loneliness, or stress, all of which are precursors to chronic diseases.

You will achieve many benefits using the Instant Pot Pressure Cooker. These are just a few instances you will discover in your Mediterranean-style recipes:

Pressure cooking means that you can (on average) cook meals 75% faster than boiling/braising on the stovetop or baking and roasting in a conventional oven.

This is especially helpful for vegan meals that entail the use of dried beans, legumes, and pulses. Instead of pre-soaking these ingredients for hours before use, you can pour them directly into the Instant Pot, add water, and pressure cook these for several minutes. However, always follow your recipe carefully since they have been tested for accuracy.

Nutrients are preserved. You can use your pressure-cooking techniques using the Instant Pot to ensure the heat is evenly and quickly distributed. It is not essential to immerse the food into the water. You will provide plenty of water in the cooker for efficient steaming. You will also be saving the essential vitamins and minerals. The food won't become oxidized by the exposure of air or heat. Enjoy those fresh green veggies with their natural and vibrant colors.

The cooking elements help keep the foods fully sealed, so the steam and aromas don't linger throughout your entire home. That is a plus, especially for items such as cabbage, which throws out a distinctive smell.

You will find that beans and whole grains will have a softer texture and will have an improved taste. The meal will be cooked consistently since the Instant Pot provides even heat distribution.

You'll also save tons of time and money. You will be using much less water, and the pot is fully insulated, making it more energy-efficient when compared to boiling or steaming your foods on the stovetop. It is also less expensive than using a microwave, not to mention how much more flavorful the food will be when prepared in the Instant Pot cooker.

You can delay the cooking of your food items so you can plan ahead of time. You won't need to stand around as you await your meal. You can reduce the cooking time by reducing the 'hands-on' time. Just leave for work or a day of activities, and you will come home to a special treat.

In a nutshell, the Instant Pot is:

Easy To Use Healthy recipes for the entire family are provided.

You can make authentic one-pot recipes in your Instant Pot.

If you forget to switch on your slow cooker, you can make any meal done in a few minutes in your Instant Pot.

You can securely and smoothly cook meat from frozen.

It's a laid-back way to cook. You don't have to watch a pan on the stove or a pot in the oven.

The pressure cooking procedure develops delicious flavors swiftly.

CPSIA information can be obtained
at www.ICGtesting.com
Printed in the USA
BVHW052032120421
604748BV00001B/46